STEPHEN SONDHEIM
BROADWAY SOLOS

CONTENTS

THE CD IS PLAYABLE ON ANY CD PLAYER, AND IS ALSO ENHANCED SO MAC AND PC USERS CAN ADJUST
THE RECORDING TO ANY TEMPO WITHOUT CHANGING THE PITCH.

ISBN 978-1-4234-7282-7

RILTING MUSIC, INC.

EXCLUSIVELY DISTRIBUTED BY

HAL•LEONARD®
CORPORATION

7777 W. BLUEMOUND RD. P.O. BOX 13819 MILWAUKEE, WI 53213

Visit Hal Leonard Online at
www.halleonard.com

ANYONE CAN WHISTLE
from ANYONE CAN WHISTLE

Words and Music by
STEPHEN SONDHEIM

TROMBONE

1/2

BEING ALIVE

from COMPANY

Music and Lyrics by
STEPHEN SONDHEIM

TROMBONE

BROADWAY BABY

from FOLLIES

Music and Lyrics by
STEPHEN SONDHEIM

TROMBONE

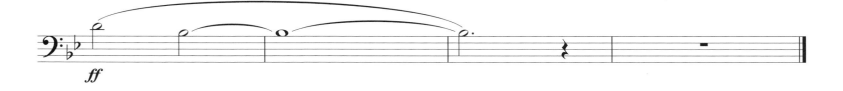

CHILDREN WILL LISTEN

from INTO THE WOODS

TROMBONE

Words and Music by
STEPHEN SONDHEIM

COMEDY TONIGHT

from A FUNNY THING HAPPENED ON THE WAY TO THE FORUM

TROMBONE

Words and Music by
STEPHEN SONDHEIM

GOOD THING GOING

from MERRILY WE ROLL ALONG

Words and Music by
STEPHEN SONDHEIM

TROMBONE

JOHANNA
from SWEENEY TODD

Words and Music by
STEPHEN SONDHEIM

TROMBONE

LOSING MY MIND

from FOLLIES

Music and Lyrics by
STEPHEN SONDHEIM

TROMBONE

NOT A DAY GOES BY

from MERRILY WE ROLL ALONG

TROMBONE

Words and Music by
STEPHEN SONDHEIM

Slowly, with feeling

NOT WHILE I'M AROUND

from SWEENEY TODD

TROMBONE

Words and Music by
STEPHEN SONDHEIM

OLD FRIENDS

from MERRILY WE ROLL ALONG

Words and Music by
STEPHEN SONDHEIM

TROMBONE

PRETTY WOMEN

from SWEENEY TODD

Words and Music by
STEPHEN SONDHEIM

TROMBONE

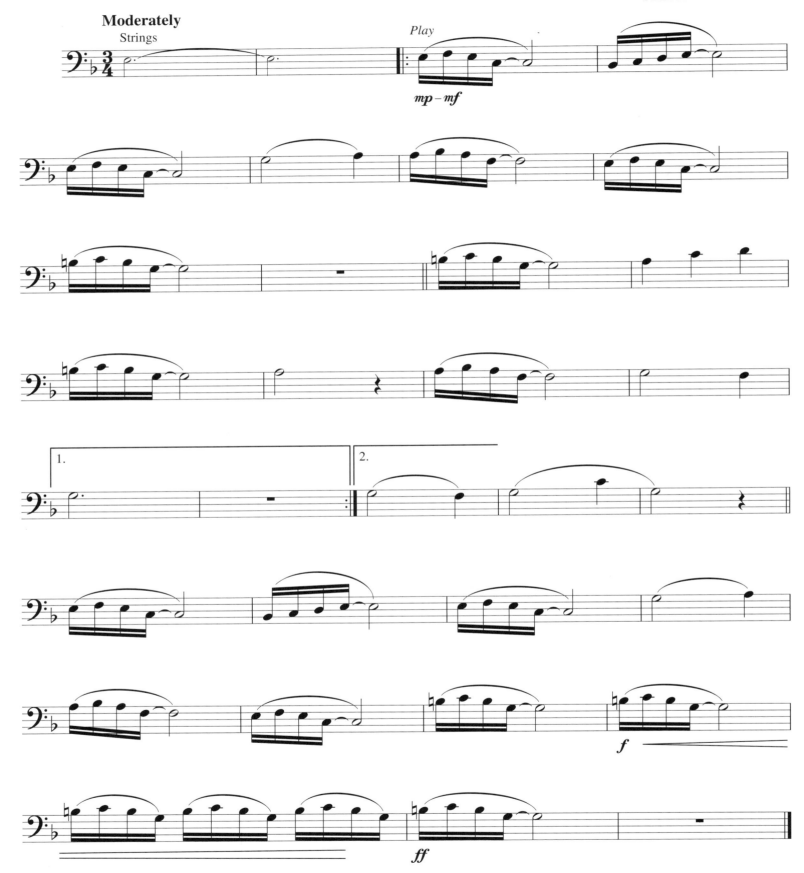

SEND IN THE CLOWNS

from the Musical A LITTLE NIGHT MUSIC

Words and Music by
STEPHEN SONDHEIM

25/26

TROMBONE

SUNDAY

from SUNDAY IN THE PARK WITH GEORGE

Words and Music by
STEPHEN SONDHEIM

TROMBONE

Slowly with feeling